Ka

by Iain Gray

Lang**Syne**
PUBLISHING
WRITING *to* REMEMBER

Lang**Syne**

PUBLISHING

WRITING *to* REMEMBER

E-mail: info@lang-syne.co.uk

Distributed in the Republic of Ireland by Portfolio Group,
Kilbarrack Ind. Est. Kilbarrack, Dublin 5.
T:00353(01) 839 4918 F:00353(01) 839 5826
sales@portfoliogroup.ie
www.portfoliogroup.ie

Design by Dorothy Meikle   Printed by Fixture Displays, China

ISBN 978-1-85217-260-2

Kavanagh

MOTTO:
Peace and plenty.

CREST:
A gold wheatsheaf.

NAME variations include:
Caomhánach *(Gaelic)*
Chaomhánach *(Gaelic)*
O'Cavanagh
Cavanagh
Cavanaugh
Kavanah
Kavanaugh
Keevan

Chapter one:
Origins of Irish surnames

**According to an old saying, there are two types of Irish –
those who actually are Irish and those who wish they were.**

This sentiment is only one example of the allure that the
high romance and drama of the proud nation's history holds
for thousands of people scattered across the world today.

It's a sad fact, however, that the vast majority of Irish
surnames are found far beyond Irish shores, rather than on
the Emerald Isle itself.

The population stood at around eight million souls in
1841, but today it stands at fewer than six million.

This is mainly a tragic consequence of the potato
famine, also known as the Great Hunger, which devastated
Ireland between 1845 and 1849.

The Irish peasantry had become almost wholly reliant
for basic sustenance on the potato, first introduced from the
Americas in the seventeenth century.

When the crop was hit by a blight, at least 800,000
people starved to death while an estimated two million
others were forced to seek a new life far from their native
shores – particularly in America, Canada, and Australia.

The effects of the potato blight continued until about
1851, by which time a firm pattern of emigration had
become established.

Ireland's loss, however, was to the gain of the countries in which the immigrants settled, contributing enormously, as their descendants do today, to the well being of the nations in which their forefathers settled.

But those who were forced through dire circumstance to establish a new life in foreign parts never forgot their roots, or the proud heritage and traditions of the land that gave them birth.

Nor do their descendants.

It is a heritage that is inextricably bound up in the colourful variety of Irish names themselves – and the origin and history of these names forms an integral part of the vibrant drama that is the nation's history, one of both glorious fortune and tragic misfortune.

This history is well documented, and one of the most important and fascinating of the earliest sources are *The Annals of the Four Masters*, compiled between 1632 and 1636 by four friars at the Franciscan Monastery in County Donegal.

Compiled from earlier sources, and purporting to go back to the Biblical Deluge, much of the material takes in the mythological origins and history of Ireland and the Irish.

This includes tales of successive waves of invaders and settlers such as the Fomorians, the Partholonians, the Nemedians, the Fir Bolgs, the Tuatha De Danann, and the Laigain.

Of particular interest are the *Milesian Genealogies*,

because the majority of Irish clans today claim a descent from either Heremon, Ir, or Heber – three of the sons of Milesius, a king of what is now modern day Spain.

These sons invaded Ireland in the second millennium B.C, apparently in fulfilment of a mysterious prophecy received by their father.

This Milesian lineage is said to have ruled Ireland for nearly 3,000 years, until the island came under the sway of England's King Henry II in 1171 following what is known as the Cambro-Norman invasion.

This is an important date not only in Irish history in general, but for the effect the invasion subsequently had for Irish surnames.

'Cambro' comes from the Welsh, and 'Cambro-Norman' describes those Welsh knights of Norman origin who invaded Ireland.

But they were invaders who stayed, inter-marrying with the native Irish population and founding their own proud dynasties that bore Cambro-Norman names such as Archer, Barbour, Brannagh, Fitzgerald, Fitzgibbon, Fleming, Joyce, Plunkett, and Walsh – to name only a few.

These 'Cambro-Norman' surnames that still flourish throughout the world today form one of the three main categories in which Irish names can be placed – those of Gaelic-Irish, Cambro-Norman, and Anglo-Irish.

Previous to the Cambro-Norman invasion of the twelfth century, and throughout the earlier invasions and settlement of those wild bands of sea rovers known as the Vikings in the eighth and ninth centuries, the population of the island was relatively small, and it was normal for a person to be identified through the use of only a forename.

But as population gradually increased and there were many more people with the same forename, surnames were adopted to distinguish one person, or one community, from another.

Individuals identified themselves with their own particular tribe, or 'tuath', and this tribe – that also became known as a clann, or clan – took its name from some distinguished ancestor who had founded the clan.

The Gaelic-Irish form of the name Kelly, for example, is Ó Ceallaigh, or O'Kelly, indicating descent from an original 'Ceallaigh', with the 'O' denoting 'grandson of.' The name was later anglicised to Kelly.

The prefix 'Mac' or 'Mc', meanwhile, as with the clans of the Scottish Highlands, denotes 'son of.'

Although the Irish clans had much in common with their Scottish counterparts, one important difference lies in what are known as 'septs', or branches, of the clan.

Septs of Scottish clans were groups who often bore an entirely different name from the clan name but were under the clan's protection.

In Ireland, septs were groups that shared the same name and who could be found scattered throughout the four provinces of Ulster, Leinster, Munster, and Connacht.

The 'golden age' of the Gaelic-Irish clans, infused as their veins were with the blood of Celts, pre-dates the Viking invasions of the eighth and ninth centuries and the Norman invasion of the twelfth century, and the sacred heart of the country was the Hill of Tara, near the River Boyne, in County Meath.

Known in Gaelic as 'Teamhar na Rí', or Hill of Kings, it was the royal seat of the 'Ard Rí Éireann', or High King of Ireland, to whom the petty kings, or chieftains, from the island's provinces were ultimately subordinate.

It was on the Hill of Tara, beside a stone pillar known as the Irish 'Lia Fáil', or Stone of Destiny, that the High Kings were inaugurated and, according to legend, this stone would emit a piercing screech that could be heard all over Ireland when touched by the hand of the rightful king.

The Hill of Tara is today one of the island's main tourist attractions.

Opposition to English rule over Ireland, established in the wake of the Cambro-Norman invasion, broke out frequently and the harsh solution adopted by the powerful forces of the Crown was to forcibly evict the native Irish from their lands.

These lands were then granted to Protestant colonists, or 'planters', from Britain.

Many of these colonists, ironically, came from Scotland and were the descendants of the original 'Scotti', or 'Scots', who gave their name to Scotland after migrating there in the fifth century A.D., from the north of Ireland.

Colonisation entailed harsh penal laws being imposed on the majority of the native Irish population, stripping them practically of all of their rights.

The Crown's main bastion in Ireland was Dublin and its environs, known as the Pale, and it was the dispossessed peasantry who lived outside this Pale, desperately striving to eke out a meagre living.

It was this that gave rise to the modern-day expression of someone or something being 'beyond the pale'.

Attempts were made to stamp out all aspects of the ancient Gaelic-Irish culture, to the extent that even to bear a Gaelic-Irish name was to invite discrimination.

This is why many Gaelic-Irish names were anglicised with, for example, and noted above, Ó Ceallaigh, or O'Kelly, being anglicised to Kelly.

Succeeding centuries have seen strong revivals of Gaelic-Irish consciousness, however, and this has led to many families reverting back to the original form of their name, while the language itself is frequently found on the fluent tongues of an estimated 90,000 to 145,000 of the island's population.

Ireland's turbulent history of religious and political strife is one that lasted well into the twentieth century, a landmark century that saw the partition of the island into the twenty-six counties of the independent Republic of

Ireland, or Eire, and the six counties of Northern Ireland, or Ulster.

Dublin, originally founded by Vikings, is now a vibrant and truly cosmopolitan city while the proud city of Belfast is one of the jewels in the crown of Ulster.

It was Saint Patrick who first brought the light of Christianity to Ireland in the fifth century A.D.

Interpretations of this Christian message have varied over the centuries, often leading to bitter sectarian conflict – but the many intricately sculpted Celtic Crosses found all over the island are symbolic of a unity that crosses the sectarian divide.

It is an image that fuses the 'old gods' of the Celts with Christianity.

All the signs from the early years of this new millennium indicate that sectarian strife may soon become a thing of the past – with the Irish and their many kinsfolk across the world, be they Protestant or Catholic, finding common purpose in the rich tapestry of their shared heritage.

Chapter two:
Saints and sinners

The Kavanaghs of today, in all the rich variety of spellings of the name, can boast a truly illustrious pedigree that stretches back through the dim mists of time to the warrior kings of the ancient Irish province of Leinster.

The Kavanagh name derives from the Gaelic Caomhánach, or Chaomhánach, indicating a follower of St. Caomhán, and this was the name given to Domhnall, or Donal, a son of the twelfth century Leinster king and progenitor of the Murphy clan Diarmait MacMurchada, or Dermot MacMurrough.

Domhnall, in keeping with Celtic custom, was fostered out at an early age for his education – in his case to a monastery dedicated to St. Caomhán in Kilcavan, in present day Co. Wexford, in the southeast of the Emerald Isle.

Off the west coast of Ireland lie the beautiful Aran Islands and it was on Inishere, the smallest of the islands, that the cult of St. Caomhán first arose – with Caomhán deriving from 'caomh', meaning gentle, or mild.

As patron saint of Inishere St. Caomhán's feast day of June 14 is recognised every year, with devotees praying at his grave, known as Caomhán's Bed, on the eve of his feast day.

According to legend the saint, when fervently prayed to over his grave, has the miraculous power of calming storms at sea.

But his devotee Domhnall's father, Dermot MacMurrough, certainly never exerted any calming influences in his lifetime – largely responsible as he was for the late twelfth century Cambro-Norman invasion and subsequent consolidation of power of the English Crown.

Twelfth century Ireland was far from being a unified nation, split up as it was into territories ruled over by squabbling chieftains such as Dermot MacMurrough, who ruled as kings in their own right – and this inter-clan rivalry worked to the advantage of the invaders.

In a series of bloody conflicts one chieftain, or king, would occasionally gain the upper hand over his rivals, and by 1156 the most powerful was Muirchertach MacLochlainn, king of the powerful O'Neills.

He was opposed by the equally powerful Rory O'Connor, king of the province of Connacht, but he increased his power and influence by allying himself with Dermot MacMurrough, king of Leinster.

MacLochlainn and MacMurrough were aware that the main key to the kingdom of Ireland was the thriving trading port of Dublin that had been established by invading Vikings, or Ostmen, in 852 A.D.

Dublin was taken by the combined forces of the Leinster and Connacht kings, but when MacLochlainn died the

Dubliners rose up in revolt and overthrew the unpopular MacMurrough.

There had certainly been no love lost between MacMurrough and the Dubliners – who had not only killed his father but as an added insult buried his corpse beside that of a dead dog.

A triumphant Rory O'Connor entered Dublin and was later inaugurated as Ard Rí, but the proud Dermott MacMurrough was not one to humbly accept defeat.

He appealed for help from England's Henry II in unseating O'Connor, an act that was to radically affect the future course of Ireland's fortunes.

The English monarch agreed to help MacMurrough, but distanced himself from direct action by delegating his Norman subjects in Wales with the task.

These ambitious and battle-hardened barons and knights had first settled in Wales following the Norman Conquest of England in 1066 and, with an eye on rich booty, plunder, and lands, were only too eager to obey their sovereign's wishes and furnish MacMurrough with aid.

MacMurrough crossed the Irish Sea to Bristol, where he rallied powerful barons such as Robert Fitzstephen and Maurice Fitzgerald to his cause, along with Gilbert de Clare, Earl of Pembroke, also known as Strongbow.

As an inducement to Strongbow, MacMurrough offered him the hand of his beautiful young daughter, Aife, in marriage, with the further sweetener to the deal that he would take over the province of Leinster on MacMurrough's death.

The mighty Norman war machine soon moved into action, and so fierce and disciplined was their onslaught on the forces of Rory O'Connor and his allies that by 1171 they had re-captured Dublin, in the name of MacMurrough, and other strategically important territories.

But Henry II began to take cold feet over the venture, realising that he may have been responsible for the creation of a powerful rival in the form of a separate Norman kingdom in Ireland.

Accordingly, he landed on the island, near Waterford, at the head of a large army in October of 1171 with the aim of curbing the power of his Cambro-Norman barons.

Protracted war between the king and his barons was averted, however, when the barons submitted to the royal will, promising homage and allegiance in return for holding the territories they had conquered in the king's name.

Henry also received the submission and homage of many of the Irish chieftains, tired as they were with internecine warfare and also perhaps realising that as long as they were rivals and not united they were no match for the powerful forces the English Crown could muster.

Dermot MacMurrough had died only a few months before Henry landed in England, and history has not been kind to this ancestor of the Kavanaghs.

The Annals of the Four Masters, for example, scathingly

note that he died 'without penance, without the body of Christ, without unction, as his evil deeds deserved.'

His main crimes, according to the annals, were to have 'brought over the Saxons', and to have plundered and burned many churches.

But MacMurrough was far from alone in the desecration of church property, while it is known that Henry II had had his avaricious eyes on Ireland for some time and that an invasion was almost inevitable at some stage – with or without an invitation.

English dominion over Ireland was ratified through the Treaty of Windsor of 1175, under the terms of which Rory O'Connor, for example, was allowed to rule territory unoccupied by the Normans in the role of a vassal of the king.

In keeping with MacMurrough's promise to him, the Norman baron Strongbow took his daughter Aife as his wife and, on MacMurrough's death, attempted to take over the kingship of the province of Leinster.

Their dead king's promises to Strongbow meant nothing to his kinsmen, however, who promptly recognised MacMurrough's eldest son Domhnall Coamhánach as their rightful chieftain, ruling from the stronghold of Ui Ceinnsealaigh, or High Kinsella.

But the powerful and haughty Strongbow was not to be thwarted – with devastating consequences for Domhnall Coamhánach, progenitor of the Kavanaghs of today.

Chapter three:
Bloodied but unbeaten

Domhnall's son was kidnapped and held hostage by Strongbow and, against all the accepted rules of what passed for diplomacy in even these dark times, the baron promptly had him executed and then hired assassins to murder his father.

This was in 1175, and further treachery on the part of the Anglo-Norman usurpers followed more than 100 years later, in 1282, when Domhnall's descendant Murtagh MacDomhnall Caomhánach was invited along with his brother Art to attend peace talks in England under terms of an amnesty.

They had not even left the Irish coast before they were pounced upon and summarily beheaded.

What followed was centuries of bitter and bloody resistance on the part of the Kavanaghs and other native Irish clans as the English Crown consolidated its iron grip on Ireland.

An indication of the harsh treatment meted out to the native Irish can be found in a desperate plea sent to Pope John XII by Roderick O'Carroll of Ely, Donald O'Neil of Ulster, and a number of other Irish chieftains in 1318.

They stated: 'As it very constantly happens, whenever an Englishman, by perfidy or craft, kills an Irishman, however noble, or however innocent, be he clergy or layman, there is no penalty or correction enforced against the person who may be guilty of such wicked murder.

'But rather the more eminent the person killed and the higher rank which he holds among his own people, so much more is the murderer honoured and rewarded by the English, and not merely by the people at large, but also by the religious and bishops of the English race.'

It is in such desperate times that heroes arise, and the Kavanaghs produced many, including the freedom fighter Art Og Kavanagh, who was assassinated in 1417 after quaffing a cup of poisoned wine that he had trustingly accepted under the rules of hospitality of the time.

Another celebrated Kavanagh hero in particular and Irish hero in general was the bold Cahir Ruadh Caomhánach, best known to posterity as Red Charlie Kavanagh.

Scotland has its legendary folk hero Rob Roy MacGregor and England has its Robin Hood – and Red Charlie Kavanagh can be seen as their Irish counterpart.

A member of the Ballyloughan and Garryhill sept of the Kavanaghs, he hailed from Ballaghmore, in Fortha, Co. Carlow, but made the Blackstairs Mountains his base for repeated forays against English settlers and the forces of the Crown.

His hideout was a near-inaccessible den beneath the Scollagh Gap, and it was from here that he carried out a campaign of guerrilla warfare.

While some of his kinsfolk were forced to surrender to the authorities and reach some kind of accommodation with them, Red Charlie was made of much sterner stuff.

He gave much of the proceeds of his raids on English settlements to not only his kinsfolk and other supporters, but also the ordinary folk who languished under English rule.

One of his kinsfolk, Cahir MacArt Kavanagh, played a leading role in two separate rebellions that swept the island from 1569 to 1573 and 1579 to 1583, while the Kavanaghs were also at the forefront of a rebellion that erupted in 1641.

This was against the English Crown's policy of settling, or 'planting' loyal Protestants on Irish land, and one of the leaders of the rebellion was Sir Morgan Kavanagh.

The policy of plantation had started during the reign from 1491 to 1547 of Henry VIII, whose Reformation effectively outlawed the established Roman Catholic faith throughout his dominions.

This settlement of loyal Protestants in Ireland continued throughout the subsequent reigns of Elizabeth I, James I (James VI of Scotland), and Charles I.

In the insurrection that exploded in 1641, at least 2,000 Protestant settlers were massacred at the hands of Catholic landowners and their native Irish peasantry, while thousands more were stripped of their belongings and driven from their lands to seek refuge where they could.

In the bitter internecine conflict, Morgan Kavanagh was killed in 1643.

Terrible as the atrocities were against the Protestant settlers, subsequent accounts became greatly exaggerated, serving to fuel a burning desire on the part of Protestants for revenge against the rebels.

Tragically for Ireland, this revenge became directed not only against the rebels, but native Irish Catholics such as the Kavanaghs in general.

The English Civil War intervened to prevent immediate action against the rebels, but following the execution of Charles I in 1649 and the consolidation of the power of England's Oliver Cromwell, the time was ripe for revenge.

The Lord Protector, as he was named, descended on Ireland at the head of a 20,000-strong army that landed at Ringford, near Dublin, in August of 1649.

The consequences of this Cromwellian conquest still resonate throughout the island today.

Cromwell had three main aims: to quash all forms of rebellion, to 'remove' all Catholic landowners who had taken part in the rebellion, and to convert the native Irish to the Protestant faith.

An early warning of the terrors that were in store for the native Catholic Irish came when the northeastern town of Drogheda was stormed and taken in September and between 2,000 and 4,000 of its inhabitants killed, including priests who were summarily put to the sword.

Sir Arthur Aston, who had refused to surrender the town, was captured and brutally clubbed to death with his wooden leg – the blood-crazed Cromwellian troopers having mistakenly believed he had stuffed it with gold pieces.

The defenders of Drogheda's St. Peter's Church, who had also refused to surrender, were burned to death as they huddled for refuge in the steeple and the church was deliberately torched.

It was not long before Cromwell held Ireland in a vice like grip, allowing him to implement what amounted to a policy of ethnic cleansing.

His troopers were given free rein to hunt down and kill priests, while Catholic estates, such as those of the Kavanaghs were confiscated.

Catholic landowners in Ulster, Leinster, and Munster were grudgingly given pathetically small estates west of the river Shannon – where they were hemmed in by colonies of Cromwellian soldiers who had been given land as reward for their military service.

Morgan Kavanagh's sons, Charles and Daniel, had played a prominent and bold role in the Cromwellian wars and, bloodied but nevertheless unbowed as far as their fierce pride was concerned, later found refuge in France and Spain.

The final death knell of the ancient Gaelic order of proud native Irish clans such as the Kavanaghs was sounded in the late seventeenth century in what is known in Ireland as Cogadh an Dá Rí, or The War of the Two Kings.

Also known as the Williamite War in Ireland or the

Jacobite War in Ireland, it was sparked off in 1688 when the Stuart monarch James II (James VII of Scotland) was deposed and fled into exile in France.

The Protestant William of Orange and his wife Mary (ironically a daughter of James II), were invited to take up the thrones of Scotland, Ireland, and England – but James still had significant support in Ireland.

His supporters were known as Jacobites, and among them was Charles Kavanagh, who returned from exile to fight for the restoration of the Stuart monarch.

Following the arrival in England of William and Mary from Holland, Richard Talbot, 1st Earl of Tyrconnell and James's Lord Deputy in Ireland, assembled an army loyal to the Stuart cause.

The aim was to garrison and fortify the island in the name of James and beat down any resistance.

Londonderry, or Derry, proved loyal to the cause of William of Orange, or William III as he had become, and managed to hold out against a siege that was not lifted until July 28, 1689.

James, with the support of troops and money supplied by Louis XIV of France, had landed at Kinsale in March of 1689 and joined forces with his Irish supporters.

A series of military encounters followed, culminating in James's defeat by an army commanded by William at the battle of the Boyne on July 12, 1689.

James fled again into French exile, never to return, while

another significant Jacobite defeat occurred in July of 1691 at the battle of Aughrim – with about half their army killed on the field, wounded, or taken prisoner.

The Williamite forces besieged Limerick and the Jacobites were forced into surrender in September of 1691.

A peace treaty, known as the Treaty of Limerick followed, under which those Jacobites willing to swear an oath of loyalty to William were allowed to remain in their native land.

Those reluctant to do so, including many native Irish such as the Kavanaghs, were allowed to seek exile on foreign shores – but their ancient homelands were lost to them forever.

A further flight overseas occurred following an abortive rebellion in 1798, while Kavanaghs were among the many thousands of Irish who were forced to seek a new life many thousands of miles from their native land during the famine known as The Great Hunger, caused by a failure of the potato crop between 1845 and 1849.

But in many cases Ireland's loss of sons and daughters such as the Kavanaghs was to the gain of those equally proud nations in which they settled.

Chapter four:
On the world stage

**Generations of Kavanaghs have flourished, and
continue to flourish, in a diverse range of pursuits – not
least the world of literature.**

Born in 1904 in Inniskeen, Co. Down, **Patrick
Kavanagh** is recognised as having been one of Ireland's
greatest poets.

His father was a farmer who managed to eke out a
precarious living by also working as a shoemaker, and these
were trades that Kavanagh himself followed when not
engaged in his literary works.

The greatest and most controversial of these was *The
Great Hunger*, a poem that attacked both the religious and
sexual repression of the Catholic Church of the time,
particularly in Kavanagh's own rural Ireland.

Other great poems with a rural theme followed, including
Tarry Flynn, *The Green Fool*, and *On Raglan Road*.

The latter poem, set to the traditional air *The Dawning
of the Day*, has been performed in recent years by artistes
who include Sinéad O'Connor, Van Morrison, Billy Bragg,
and Mark Knopfler.

One of the many admirers of his work worldwide,
meanwhile, is the Australian actor Russell Crowe.

Kavanagh died in 1967, but Patrick Kavanagh weekend

talks are held every November in his birthplace of Inniskeen, while there is a fine statue of him beside Dublin's majestic Grand Canal.

His brother, **Dr. Peter Kavanagh**, born in Inniskeen in 1916 and who died in 2006, was the scholar and writer who was responsible for collecting and publishing his works.

Born in 1954, **Ed Kavanagh** is the multi-talented Newfoundland and Labrador writer, teacher, and musician who penned the popular *Amanda Greenleaf* series of children's books.

A gifted harpist, he also performs traditional Newfoundland music.

Best known for her short stories, **Herminie T. Kavanagh**, born in 1859, was the Irish-American author whose second husband, **Marcus Kavanagh**, served for a time as a judge in Cook County, Illinois, while **Julia Kavanagh**, born in 1824 in Thurles, Co. Tipperary, was also a noted author.

Her father, **Morgan Kavanagh**, wrote widely on the source and science of languages while she herself became an expert on examining and writing about the French way of life.

It was over the course of many trips to France that she penned works such as *Women in France during the Eighteenth Century*, *French Women of Letters*, and the novels *The Three Paths* and *Madeleine: A Tale of Auvergne*.

Kavanaghs have also excelled in the world of art, most

notably the Irish **Joseph Kavanagh**, born in 1856 and who died in 1918.

A friend and contemporary of the artist Walter Osborne, he studied at Dublin's Metropolitan School of Art and in Antwerp.

Before returning to his native land he produced numerous paintings of Antwerp and its countryside in addition to landscape paintings of Brittany, in France.

Sadly, many of his paintings were later destroyed in an accidental fire in Dublin.

Kavanaghs have also been prominent in the often-cutthroat world of politics.

Born in 1866 in Green County, Alabama, **William Kavanaugh** was a Democratic United States Senator for Arkansas, while **Jack Kavanagh** was leader of the Socialist Party of Canada from 1908 to 1921.

A founding member of the Communist Party of Canada, he moved to Australia in 1925 and for the next five years was a leader of the Australian Communist Party.

Born in 1795 in Lincoln County, Maine, **Edward Kavanagh** practised law before pursuing a political career that included election to the Maine State Senate and his appointment to a diplomatic post in Portugal by American President Andrew Jackson.

Brett Kavanaugh, born in Washington D.C. in 1965 is the former Staff Secretary in the Executive Office of the President of the United States who, at the time of writing, is a federal judge in the United States Court of Appeals for the District of Columbia Circuit.

Born in 1941, **Dennis Kavanagh** is an influential British political analyst and author who, at the time of writing, is professor of politics at Liverpool University.

In the world of contemporary music **Niamh Kavanagh**, born in 1968, is the Irish singer who, in addition to providing both some of the lead and backing vocals for the soundtrack for the film *The Commitments*, won the Eurovision Song Contest for her country in 1993 with the song *Singing In Your Eyes*.

Born in 1964, **Chris Kavanagh** is the British drummer who has played for iconic bands such as Sigue Sigue Sputnik and Big Audio Dynamite II.

In the highly competitive sports arena, **Pat Kavanagh**, born in Ottawa in 1979, is the Canadian professional ice hockey player who, at the time of writing, plays for the Iserlohn Roosters in the German hockey league.

He has also played for teams that include the Vancouver Canucks, the Kansas City Blades, and the Philadelphia Flyers.

Born in 1923, **Ken Kavanagh** is the former motorcycle road racer and racecar driver who in 1952 became the first Australian to win a motorcycle Grand Prix race when he won the 350cc Ulster Grand Prix.

Another **Ken Kavanagh**, born in 1916 in Little Rock, Arkansas, and who died in January of 2007, was the noted American football player, coach, and scout who was elected to America's College Football Hall of Fame in 1963.

He also had a distinguished war record as a pilot, flying no less than 30 missions during the Second World War and being awarded the Distinguished Flying Cross and the Air Medal with four oak leaf clusters.

Born in 1821 in Mullingar, Co. Westmeath, **Thomas Henry Kavanagh** holds the distinction of being one of only five civilians ever to have been awarded the Victoria Cross – the highest award for gallantry for British and Commonwealth military personnel.

He had been in the service of the Bengal Civil Service during the Indian Mutiny when, at Lucknow in November of 1857 he volunteered to go through the besieged city to the camp of the relieving forces.

Cunningly disguised, he managed to slip through the ranks of the mutineers and, reaching the camp, was able to guide a body of troops back to the besieged garrison and enable it to be relieved.

He died five years later in Gibraltar and his grave can be seen to this day in Gibraltar's North Front Cemetery.

On the stage **Anthony Kavanagh Jr.** is the Canadian actor, singer, and comedian who was born in Quebec in 1969 to parents who had found asylum in Canada from the political repression of their native Haiti.

Now a popular star in France as host of his own television show, he previously played Billy Flynn in the musical *Chicago* in Montreal.

On a rather infamous note, **Lawrence Kavanagh**, born in about 1805 in Waterford, was destined to end his life on the gallows in Australia, far from his native Ireland.

Convicted of burglary in Dublin in 1828 he was sentenced to transportation for life, and his career thereafter was a dramatic and colourful catalogue of violent brushes with the authorities, imprisonment, escape, further imprisonment and even further daring escape.

A notorious outlaw, but one who nevertheless captured the romantic imagination of Australians in the same manner as the equally infamous Ned Kelly, he was finally run to ground and hanged in October of 1846.

One of Ireland's most enlightened politicians of the nineteenth century was **Arthur MacMorrough Kavanagh**, born in Co. Carlow in 1831.

A descendant of the ancient and illustrious Kings of Leinster, he overcame severe physical disadvantages to become not only a noted landowner, politician, and philanthropist, but also a sportsman and artist.

Born with only the rudiments of arms and legs, he nevertheless was able to ride, hunt, shoot, and fish and undertake often arduous journeys throughout India, Egypt, and what is now modern day Iran.

He was the Conservative Member of Parliament (M.P.) for Co. Wexford from 1866 to 1868, and later an M.P. for Co. Carlow. He died in 1889.

Key dates in Ireland's history from the first settlers to the formation of the Irish Republic:

circa 7000 B.C.	Arrival and settlement of Stone Age people.
circa 3000 B.C.	Arrival of settlers of New Stone Age period.
circa 600 B.C.	First arrival of the Celts.
200 A.D.	Establishment of Hill of Tara, Co. Meath, as seat of the High Kings.
circa 432 A.D.	Christian mission of St. Patrick.
800-920 A.D.	Invasion and subsequent settlement of Vikings.
1002 A.D.	Brian Boru recognised as High King.
1014	Brian Boru killed at battle of Clontarf.
1169-1170	Cambro-Norman invasion of the island.
1171	Henry II claims Ireland for the English Crown.
1366	Statutes of Kilkenny ban marriage between native Irish and English.
1529-1536	England's Henry VIII embarks on religious Reformation.
1536	Earl of Kildare rebels against the Crown.
1541	Henry VIII declared King of Ireland.
1558	Accession to English throne of Elizabeth I.
1565	Battle of Affane.
1569-1573	First Desmond Rebellion.
1579-1583	Second Desmond Rebellion.
1594-1603	Nine Years War.
1606	Plantation' of Scottish and English settlers.

1607	Flight of the Earls.
1632-1636	Annals of the Four Masters compiled.
1641	Rebellion over policy of plantation and other grievances.
1649	Beginning of Cromwellian conquest.
1688	Flight into exile in France of Catholic Stuart monarch James II as Protestant Prince William of Orange invited to take throne of England along with his wife, Mary.
1689	William and Mary enthroned as joint monarchs; siege of Derry.
1690	Jacobite forces of James defeated by William at battle of the Boyne (July) and Dublin taken.
1691	Athlone taken by William; Jacobite defeats follow at Aughrim, Galway, and Limerick; conflict ends with Treaty of Limerick (October) and Irish officers allowed to leave for France.
1695	Penal laws introduced to restrict rights of Catholics; banishment of Catholic clergy.
1704	Laws introduced constricting rights of Catholics in landholding and public office.
1728	Franchise removed from Catholics.
1791	Foundation of United Irishmen republican movement.
1796	French invasion force lands in Bantry Bay.
1798	Defeat of Rising in Wexford and death of United Irishmen leaders Wolfe Tone and Lord Edward Fitzgerald.

1800	Act of Union between England and Ireland.
1803	Dublin Rising under Robert Emmet.
1829	Catholics allowed to sit in Parliament.
1845-1849	The Great Hunger: thousands starve to death as potato crop fails and thousands more emigrate.
1856	Phoenix Society founded.
1858	Irish Republican Brotherhood established.
1873	Foundation of Home Rule League.
1893	Foundation of Gaelic League.
1904	Foundation of Irish Reform Association.
1913	Dublin strikes and lockout.
1916	Easter Rising in Dublin and proclamation of an Irish Republic.
1917	Irish Parliament formed after Sinn Fein election victory.
1919-1921	War between Irish Republican Army and British Army.
1922	Irish Free State founded, while six northern counties remain part of United Kingdom as Northern Ireland, or Ulster; civil war up until 1923 between rival republican groups.
1949	Foundation of Irish Republic after all remaining constitutional links with Britain are severed.